SO-BUC-696

the little black book of **more dating ideas**

VOLUME 2

a buzz boxx book

John Graham / Stuart Ough

Andrews and McMeel
A Universal Press Syndicate Company
Kansas City

The Little Black Book of More Dating Ideas, Volume 2 copyright © 1997 by buzz boxx. Cover copyright ® 1997 by buzz boxx. All rights reserved. Printed in the United States of America. No part of this book may be used or reproduced in any manner whatsoever without written permission except in the case of reprints in the context of reviews. For information, write Andrews and McMeel, a Universal Press Syndicate Company, 4520 Main Street, Kansas City, Missouri 64111.

ISBN 0-8362-2753-0

Library of Congress Catalog Card Number: 96-86659

ATTENTION: SCHOOLS AND BUSINESSES

Andrews and McMeel books are available at quantity discounts with bulk purchase for educational, business, or sales promotional use. For information, please write to: Special Sales Department, Andrews and McMeel, 4520 Main Street, Kansas City, Missouri 64111

buzz boxx

Who are we?

the lost generation . . . slackers . . . generation x . . . whiners . . . whatever. welcome to buzz boxx.

buzz boxx is a product company of, for, and about young people. buzz boxx is made up of talented young people from various backgrounds who create, make, and sell products intended for our peers. sorry, no big 50-year-old v.p. of marketing trying to dictate what we should like and buy. after all, we know what we like best. it's a means for us to express ourselves in a positive way and bring some smiles to people's faces. remember, life is way too short. make a positive difference by what you do in the world around you.

we're buzz boxx – the voice of young america

Book design by buzz boxx and Morgan Taylor.

Photos by Greg Whitaker.

Thanks to Back Home Indiana at Circle Centre Mall in Indianapolis for allowing us to photograph in the store. More thanks to MORE "dating dilemma" friends who willingly mugged for the camera. Their names are listed at the back of this book.

more
intro

As we return you to the saga from our first dating ideas book, our hero, the lonely single person struggling desperately to answer life's big question, "I don't know, what do you want to do?" is well . . . still single and on occasion still lapsing into the old routine, struggling to answer that question. But no matter! Swooping down from the skies to save the day (or weekend) is *The Little Black Book of MORE Dating Ideas, Volume 2.* Back and better than ever with MORE unique, refreshing, creative, and off-the-wall ideas for the next time you go out to do battle with the evil forces of boredom, complacency, or lack of creative brain charge.

An overwhelming response by readers, many of you who even sent in ideas of your own, demanded MORE and sealed our fate—to create a series that will rid us all of that fateful question and save the planet!

What's wrong with making decisions more simple and life more exciting? Nothing, that's what! So, grab your date. Get your friends together. (And HELLO married people, you still SHOULD go on dates with your spouse.) Have a little fun with it. NO! Have A LOT of fun with it. We know we did.

And until next time, thanks and happy dating.

buzz boxx

P.S. If you have EVEN MORE dating ideas that you'd like to tell us about, we'd still like to hear from you. Yep, you guessed it, we had EVEN MORE ideas than we could use in this book so we're already writing *The Little Black Book of EVEN MORE Dating Ideas, Volume 3* (groovy title, hunh?!). See the last page for details.

more contents

What about something that's more simple & easy........1

Well, I have more ideas that are different & free.....23

I'm in the mood for something more romantic & thoughtful...43

Hey! Let's do something more off the wall.........61

Don't worry about it, I've got more money to burn.........81

It's easy to come up with more ideas with a change of seasons...97

Sometimes I like dates more that are group gatherings.....111

What about something that's

more
simple &
easy

Buy a copy of this book for your date. Call out any page number. Choose one of the ideas from the selected page and just do it.

No fighting over who's William Tell and who gets to put the apple on their head. Go to an archery range and aim for the bull's-eye instead.

Here's a way to think about each other every 3,000 miles. Take a basic auto maintenance class together. Get dirty as you check each other's oil.

Baby-sit together for family or friends. Test your mettle to see if kids are in your future.

Tour a bakery and sample a variety of fresh baked breads. Yummy!

Hey dere. For cripes' sake, drive to a dairy farm and take a tour. When you're finished buy some fresh cheese curds or string cheese.

Go bicycling. Better yet, rent a bicycle built for two.

Give to those in need. Donate blood together and then go out for a big dinner afterward.

Imagine life on the open sea together and walk around a boat show.

Don't just gawk from a distance. Take a canyon tour or trail tour on horseback or mules.

Ever wonder how your autos are born? Shift gears and tour a car factory.

Play cards. How many card games do you know? Teach each other new card games for those rainy days. Bridge anyone?

Take puzzles and mysteries into the next generation. Challenge your thinking abilities as you play an interactive CD-ROM game like *Myst* or the irreverent *You Don't Know Jack*.

Sing in a church choir together.

Can't decide which restaurant to go to? Buy a local merchants' coupon book. Yank out all the restaurant coupons and put them in a jar. Pick one each time you can't decide where to go.

Gather the gang for a backyard croquet tournament. How about a tall glass of lemonade before your ball gets knocked outta here?

So it's not the Sahara. Take a Jeep ride in the desert.

Got two left feet? That's okay. Have fun dancing anyway. Learn how to shag, clog, or other regional kinds of dances.

Red rover, red rover, send Fido right over. Wash your dog at a dog wash together.

Head downtown and enjoy the sights. Listen to the street musicians, watch the street performers, and haggle with the variety of street vendors.

Schedule high tea with each other @ 4:00 pm just like our friends across the Atlantic. Serve scones, clotted cream, and of course a cuppa.

Bowling getting too easy for you? Try your hand at duck pin bowling.

No spinning! Play foosball or challenge another couple for the World Foosball Championship of the Milky Way Galaxy.

If the big animals are too much for you, head to a petting zoo.

Call up a mutual friend you haven't talked to in years. Go out to lunch and catch up.

Nothing to wear? Go to a garage sale and assemble an ensemble for each other. Agree to wear it on your next date.

Ying . . . no, yang? Work on your hand dexterity with Chinese medicine balls, any hand puzzles such as a Rubik's cube, or any of those annoying little metal ring puzzles that you can't get apart.

Fore! Head to the driving range and see who can whack
their Titilus the farthest.

Any good with the rock? Play a few games of H-O-R-S-E
or Around-the-World at a local basketball court.

Get cultured by attending an ethnic festival in your
area—Greek, Italian, German, Polish, etc.

Get your motor runnin' . . .
take a one-tank trip and go for a weekend drive.

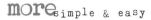

Stretch your legs and your best friend's paws.
Walk the dog together. If you don't have one,
borrow a friend's.

Go to a living history museum. Watch people in period
costumes relive life as it once was.

Look out! . . . Zap! . . . Ping! . . . Hey! . . . Whoa! . . .
AAaargh, hand cramp! Sound like fun? It is!
It's Sega-fest! If you don't own a game machine,
rent one at the local video store along with
several games and play all day.

Yee-haw! Learn how to square dance or go two-stepping. Many country bars offer free lessons early in the evening.

Is it haunted? Tour stately old mansions open to the public and see how the wealthy once lived.

So maybe you won't become Michelangelo. Enroll in an art class together like ceramics, sculpture, or sketching.

Not ready for a full-size hog? Hop on some minibikes at a nearby dirt track.

Find an out-of-the-way place for some swimming and just hanging out. Start with an old abandoned quarry.

It's a random dinner!
Open a cookbook to a random page and wherever you land, prepare the item(s) for dinner. Tasty.

Rack 'em up and shoot some pool.

Look for an old, giant tractor tire. Build a swing for two
or just roll each other down a long sloping hill.

Stroke . . . stroke . . . learn how to row a tandem scull.
. . . Stroke . . . stroke.

Rumba, tango, samba, and mambo. Take a Latin dance
class together. Aye chi wowa!

In one month go through the alphabet. Rent movies from
A to Z.

Work it—two-three-four. Get fit together. Take an aerobics
class.

Get fit together with the latest exercise craze. Go to a
spinning class together.

For some real monkey business, go to the zoo.

Wash and wax
your cars together
on a bright sunny
day. Just be sure
to be the one
with the hose!

On a sunny day, spread out an old blanket and sunbathe together. Listen to some tunes and just hang. Don't forget the sunscreen!

Enjoy an airboat ride through a swamp or marshland. And please, keep your hands and feet inside during the ride.

Look, it's Sir Edmund Hillary! Head for the mountains and do some climbing, trekking, or rappelling. For city slickers, check out a sporting goods store or health club with indoor walls you can climb.

Set your sights on the future. Stroll through a home-a-rama or home show that showcases interior designers in your area.

Rent a "year" of movies. Pick a year and rent only movies from that year. Start with your birth year.

Express your opinions. Vote. Research the candidates and head to the polls together.

Surf the Web. Travel to distant lands,
shop for unique items, and meet new and
interesting people, and be home in time for dinner.
(Hey, e-mail us at buzzboxx@aol.com).

Buy our first book,
The Little Black Book of Dating Ideas,
and start on page 1
(okay, an obvious plug).

Well, I have

more ideas that are

different & free

For years you've both watched it from the couch. Change your view and become audience members for the taping of a favorite TV show.

For something truly spiritual and thought-provoking, read passages from the *Bible*, the *Koran*, the *Torah*, etc. Or join a local prayer group.

Bring a smile to a young child's face. Volunteer to be a Big Brother or Big Sister. How about a Big Couple?

Excuse me, can you tell me where the cookbooks are?
Oh you're authors, not store employees. Attend a book
signing party at a local bookstore. Check out your
newspaper's calendar for listings. Look for
buzz boxx appearing at a store near you.
We look like clerks, not authors.

Willkommen ya. Shuren yoo vant to know how da beer is
made, so go take un tour of da brewery nearest yoo und
sample da beers. Prost!

Feeling a little outgoing? Go to a casting call together.
Who knows, you might just get "discovered."

Test love's endurance. Enter a mini-marathon and train for it together.

Going to the chapel and you're . . . gonna take a tour. Cathedrals and temples are some of the most beautiful structures in the world with much to tell. Take a tour and see the stained-glass windows, art, and mosaics. Explore the history on the walls during nonservice hours. Why not say a prayer while you're there?

Dress and act like a celebrity for a day. Wear sunglasses even inside. Hang out where other celebrities like to go.

Watch a live landing or takeoff of the shuttle. Listen for the sonic boom as it enters the Earth's atmosphere.

Chinese fire drill! Stop the car! Everyone, switch positions!

Head to America's store, Wal-Mart. Set a budget, fill a cart, and see who finds the most novel stuff . . . just like the couple who submitted this dating idea.

Put a sure smile on
someone's face. Adopt a
grandparent together. Go
to a nursing home to
visit, or play cards,
bingo, or other games on
a regular basis.

They say the way to win a woman's heart is with a box of chocolates. Tour a chocolate factory together and see what a whole factory does!

Coach a youth sports team together for a season. Hey, hey, shoot at the other goal!

Creepy crawlies! Go night crawling, look for bugs and roly-polies under rocks with flashlights. Eeewww!

In the corporate world they say the first one to the top wins. Test that theory with your own elevator races! Loser buys.

Watch Cindy, Tyra, Linda, and Kate strut their stuff at a high-fashion show. (Then try to figure out if people would actually wear it?!)

Vanna, we'd like to buy a vowel please. Try out for a game show together. Let's try "More Dating Ideas" for 1,000.

Try your hand at amateur geology and check out the lay of the land. Go for a walk along a creek, river, or canal and see how many kinds and colors of rocks you can find.

What's that shining in the dark? A ghost? A UFO? No it's a glow-in-the-dark ball! Enjoy a game of night catch or kick ball, and watch your step!

Save the planet. Make greeting cards, birthday cards, or holiday cards by reusing materials in your home.

Attempt some Haiku. (5 syllables)
It is for some though not all. (7 syllables)
Give Haiku a try. (5 syllables)

Whoomp, crash, thunder, whirl! Watch heavy construction
machinery in action.

Become a part of history. Join a historical preservation or
reenactment society today.

What a ringer of an idea. Throw a game of horseshoes.

What's it like to be Elizabeth Taylor? Search for the most expensive piece of jewelry, try it on, and you'll find out.

Do a jigsaw puzzle. Once you've mastered that go up and out, try a 3-d puzzle.

Hee . . . hee . . . teehee . . . teeheehee . . . GUFFAW! Tell jokes to each other and see who's the first one to crack.

Take a stroll down memory lane. Pull out your old junior high, high school, or college yearbooks. Dig that Farrah Fawcett 'do.

Looking for distant pen pals together? Send a message in a bottle or tied to a balloon.

Here's a cheap getaway to foreign lands. Spend Sunday morning reading a newspaper from a foreign city. Look for one at your local newsstand or even a grocery store.

Pose as millionaires for the day. Schedule a showing or attend an open house of a million-dollar home and gawk.

Expand yourself, warriors. Learn origami, the Japanese art of folding paper into shapes and animals. Can you make a grasshopper, grasshoppers?

Take an old picture frame and redecorate it together. Get creative, get kitschy, and have fun.

Tired of your place? Redecorate and rearrange your home together. Do the unexpected for a change and break those silly norms that govern where to place furniture and hang pictures.

It's refrigerator potpourri! Make an entire meal using leftovers or surprise foods in the fridge, especially the ones wrapped in aluminum foil.

Find out more about yourselves. Check out the book *Do What You Are* and take the personality tests to determine the type of career that's ideal for each other. Is it time for career changes? Help each other rewrite your résumé if it is. (Hey, we may be rewriting ours if this book doesn't sell.)

Play Ping-Pong. Ping . . . Pong . . . Ping . . . Pong . . .

Whoever said education couldn't be free? Crash a giant university lecture hall with an interesting subject (and billions of students).

Want to know what life's like for your companion?
Reverse roles for the weekend and find out. If they
usually do the asking out, why don't you?

Write each other secret code messages. Use invisible ink.

Write a short story together. Make it a mystery, romance,
fiction, or anything you wish. Try to have it published in
a newspaper, magazine, or book. Post it on-line.

Scoot on over and play some shuffleboard.

So maybe it won't be O.J. on the stand, but it might be more interesting. Spend the day in court. Attend a trial.

Wonder how shows appear on your magic box at home? Tour a TV station together and get a behind-the-scenes look.

Be amateur anthropologists. Explore a vacant building, house, or school in the country. Try to imagine it during its heyday.

Those boots were made for walking. Put on your walking shoes and take a walking tour of your city or town. Get lost!

Unwind and reenergize, take a midday siesta together.

Are your shins aching or your joints stiff? Make it a contest and guess tomorrow's weather or high temperature without watching TV. Have a prize for the person who comes closest.

I'm in the mood for something a little

more
romantic &
thoughtful

Does your date travel a lot? Greet them at the airport, have a sign with their name on it, a limo and chauffeur waiting, and a night of "welcome home" stuff already planned.

Park in a romantic area next to a regional airport where you can see the runway lights. Bring a radio that you can tune in to the air traffic control tower frequency. Listen and watch the planes land.

Buy or build a bird feeder and attract some love birds of your own.

Take the edge off after a long week and relax at a martini bar or comfortable lounge. Find a place that's dark, has couches instead of chairs, and is not frequented by poseurs.

Create a romantic gift basket you can enjoy together. Include scented candles, wines, perfumes, lotions, chocolates, music, etc. Oo-la-la.

Stop traffic. Rent a billboard to ask your date out, or even bigger, an aerial banner from a plane. Coincide the timing with whatever you're doing outdoors.

Bake a cake in the shape of a heart or
one that spells L-O-V-E.

Have a candlelight picnic at night. Try it in your backyard
or on a rooftop.

Create your own coupon book. "This coupon entitles
bearer to a great time doing . . ." Now instead of asking,
you can redeem a coupon. No questions asked.

Spend the evening on a dinner cruise on a lake,
reservoir, or the ocean.

Be creative and slip a note or prize into a Cracker Jacks box or make fortune cookies with your own personal messages.

Jump ship. Take a weekend cruise together.

Not hungry for dinner? Go out just for dessert.

Write e-mail messages and schedule them to be sent at timed intervals. Now your date can have messages waiting to greet them in the morning at work, or at home after a challenging day.

Add some spice to your lives! Grocery shop for exotic or ethnic foods that neither one has ever had and make a meal. Look for an ethnic grocery store in your area.

Climb the fence and have a midnight picnic in an empty high school football stadium. Watch the hands so you don't get called for offsides!

Make friendship bracelets and trade them with each other.

Here's another idea to do under a full moon. Go to the beach and sit on the lifeguard stand. Howl at the moon. AAAOOOO!

Show them your good side at Glamour Shots and have a makeover and portraits done. Give it as a gift.

Visit a public golf course after dusk. Enjoy the serene quietness and landscaping. Play a little game by searching for lost balls.

Remember the old, "Will you go steady with me" ID bracelets? Engrave new ones with both of your initials. Keep it with you when you're apart. It's official—you're now going steady.

Make sweet music. Play an instrument or take lessons. Play the guitar or try a duet on the piano.

Keep 'em guessing. Send letters to your date from a "secret admirer." Mail them to distant post offices and ask the post offices to postmark the letter and send it. What a way to keep your date on their toes.

Learn how to really touch each other. Take a massage class together.

Pull out your Dayrunners and schedule an entire month of dates together . . . and <u>pen</u> it in.

For those who work the night shift, pick your date up after work with a bottle of wine and a can of oysters. Heat the oysters using the car's defroster. Enjoy the silence of the night in a parking lot . . . just like the couple who submitted this idea.

Leave surprise notes each day for an entire week before your date's birthday, your anniversary, Valentine's Day, or just because you like to do the unexpected. Hide them along with tokens of your affection for big bonus points.

Flip through your music collections to find and designate "your song."

Create a mood room in your apartment or home. Hang dark, velvet curtains. Use soft lighting. Fill it with overstuffed chairs or even bean bags. Relax and just chill.

Can't cook worth beans? Hire a personal chef to cook a romantic dinner for two.

Take your picnic to new heights—picnic in a tree! If you're lucky you may find one that hangs over water for added ambience. Bring food, a blanket, some candles, and enjoy.

Design the ultimate vacation. Research your destination, choose your activities, select your accommodations, and make it your goal in life to go together someday.

Rent classic romantic movies like *Casablanca*, *Cyrano de Bergerac* (the 1950s original), and *Romeo and Juliet*.

Show them you really care. Fill a room with flowers, stuffed animals, or balloons.

Be creative with flowers. Buy a single rose for each day for 12 straight days. Attach a note giving a single reason why you like your date. After 12 days, voilà, you have an entire bouquet and 12 cool reasons why your date is the best.

For a taste of Italy right here at home, rent a rowboat and have a friend row it for you, just like the gondolas in Venice.

Gather seashells by the seashore. (Now say it real fast.)

Heaven may be just a step away. Add a sense of surrealism to your living room. Cover everything in white sheets and hang white lights for stars.

Paint stars on your ceiling with glow-in-the-dark paint. Turn off the lights and . . .

Go all-out. Rent a meeting center's stage complete with props, special effects, and lighting to coincide with the mood. Use it to announce something really big to your date.

Watch the sunset at the beach sitting around a bonfire.

Paint the town red. Dress up and go out for a romantic night of drinks, dinner, and dancing.
Rent a limo . . . just because.

We think you will. We think you will. Take a train ride together to wherever. Do a day trip.

Explore your parent's vinyl LP collection together. Listen to a whole era of swingin' music (Dean Martin, Herb Alpert, Peggy Lee, etc.). You may be surprised at what you like. Yeah, maybe your parents are cool after all.

Do whatever your date wants to do one weekend. Do whatever you want the next.

Show up unexpectedly with a bottle of wine, a loaf of bread, and a single red rose. Oh, ma cherie amour.

Write down simple wishes you each have and seal each one in its own envelope. Trade envelopes with your partner. Open one envelope when the spirit moves you and make each other's wishes come true.

Visit Niagara Falls, Old Faithful, the Grand Canyon, or any other national natural wonder or park. This land is your land, this land is my land . . .

Hey! Let's do something

Mix your seasons up a bit. In the middle of the summer, turn up the air conditioner to high. When the house is cold and feels like winter, build a romantic fire.

Be aloof poseurs, dress in all black, and go to an art film house showing the best in independent movies.

Create a custom banner declaring your feelings for your partner. Hang it outside your home for the whole world to see!

Throw a birthday party, but pretend you're a different age. Be different and celebrate a 21st birthday when you turn 30.

Test your senses. Try to eat a meal wearing blindfolds. No peeking!

Use a glow-in-the-dark ball for a game of midnight bowling! Set up sturdy flashlights for pins and aim for the light at the end of the tunnel.

A Caesar Party for two, please. Complete your evening with togas, grapes, Caesar salad, Little Caesars Pizza, and a Sid Caesar epic. Et tu, Brute?

Create your own cartoon festival or attend an international cartoon festival held in larger cities.

Tic-toc. Build a clock. Find an unfinished clock or a clock construction set and put it together. You'll be able to enjoy your work for quite some . . . time!
(Ugh, that was bad.)

Enjoy a "Spaghetti Western" Night. Fix a giant bowl of noodles and watch those old Italian Western classics. This town ain't big enough for the two of you. Now git.

You have that special song, now create a special cocktail that becomes "your" drink together. Sip it through silly straws and enjoy.

Enroll in a computer course. What a great way to "log-in" with each other. (We know, another really bad pun.)

For a long-distance date or relationship, go to the same movie at about the same time, even though you're miles apart. Call each other up afterward on the phone or cellular. (This worked for Bill Gates.)

For a refreshing blast, rent a convertible in the winter. Crank up the heat and drive with the top down.

We know you're kids at heart so plan an entire date of kid stuff. Start with a story hour at the library or bookstore. Romp around at your nearest Discovery Zone. And say, Chuck E. Cheese please!

Want to see the world for cheap? Fly to Europe or any continent together for a licensed courier service. Bon voyage!

Here's an offbeat way to watch movies. Create your own drive-in theater. Place your TV in the backyard, spread a blanket on the ground, and watch movies under the stars. Pass the popcorn please!

Get a little groovy. Get a little funky. Get down. Make up a dance routine based on your personalities. Be sure to take turns as you both add new steps in the sequence.

Sail across a dry lake bed on a desert wind runner together.

Are you picky eaters? Break out by having an Exotic Fare Night. On your own, find really weird stuff such as escargots, pickled pig's feet, black pudding, chocolate covered ants, etc. Sample the items, but don't tell until after it's all gone.

When you're done with your siesta, have a fiesta! Buy a piñata and fill it with Hershey's Hugs and Kisses.

B-movies are art too . . . well, maybe. Enjoy them at a Bad Movie Party. Choose an actor or actress known for these movies and rent a series. Your video clerk can help you here. Look for the straight-to-video movies.

It's Picasso! Forget the brush and become one with your paint and canvas and finger paint together.

Learn about each other's past. Investigate your genealogies. See how far back you can go.

Vroom. Vroom. Start your engines and rent go-carts.

If you both like tinkering with tools, build a go-cart or soap box derby car. Drivers, start your engines.

Give yourselves CB "handles" and head for a greasy spoon or even a truck stop for a completely different eating atmosphere. That's a big 10-4, Teddy Bears.

Learn about your heraldry. Research where your ancestors come from and try to find your family's crest or crest for the region . . . just like Stuart and Christine, who submitted this idea.

It's humanitarian hunting. NO GUNS! Walk through a farmer's field in autumn and see what kinds of animals you can spot—rabbits, quails, pheasants, etc. Keep score.

Experience sensory overload in the Cadillac of all theaters, an IMAX theater.

Spend the evening playing old "getting to know you" games like Spin the Bottle, Truth or Dare, or 7 Minutes in Heaven.

Take a chance on love. Buy a lottery ticket together. Fantasize about what you'd do if you won. Watch the drawing on TV together.

See what the other side of life sees. Do a 180-degree makeover on each other. If you're normally the Brooks Brothers type, do the opposite, go grunge. Pick clothes for each other ahead of time and agree to wear them for the night.

Hark soothe forth. Hither thee to a medieval restaurant for thine repast. (Translation: Check out a medieval restaurant).

Want something spicy, hot, tasty, and healthy? Check out a Mongolian BBQ restaurant with giant woks and bamboo stirrers. Load up and choose your own ingredients.

A movie with rules, rules. Add new twists to those old movies. Make up rules before you go. For example, when a particular character appears everyone stands and salutes. You get the picture.

Hide-and-seek in the dark getting too difficult? New twist, play it wearing night-vision goggles.

Create a mystery date. Compile coupons of things you've never done before. Plan it from beginning to end and when to be ready. After you've created several, put them in identical envelopes. Next time you're stuck for an idea, pick one.

If you're both feeling enlightened, attend an open mike poetry reading. Share some of your original poems with the audience.

The drive-in cheap seats. Find a spot outside the drive-in where you can see. Bring a picnic basket filled with food and watch for free.

"Do you believe in love at first sight, or do I have to walk by you again?" Buy our hilarious book, *Pick-up Lines . . . The Best and Worst on Planet Earth.* Make a game of it. See who's the first to turn red or laugh. (Okay, another obvious plug, but can you blame us?!)

Immortalize yourself for each other. Make plaster casts or even bronze favorite body parts like a mask of your face, tush, hands, or whatever.

Squeeze yourself through some caves and caverns. Go spelunking. Is that a stalactite or stalagmite?

Challenge your friends to a public transportation race and see who takes the longest. Pick a final destination. Each group must take at least three different modes of public transportation. Last group there is the big "L."

You didn't hear this one from us. Do some movie surfing.
Head to the nearest megaplex movie theater with
18 gazillion screens. Sneak in to the movies for free.
Hide in the bathrooms between showings. It's all
in good fun, right?!

Go to a sports event in black tie and formal wear.

Go alternative! Get a tattoo together or pierce a body
part. Buy a pair of earrings and split 'em.

Recapture your childhood with a Toy Party. Rent *Toy Story* and play childhood games like the Hokey Pokey, Duck-Duck-Goose, Candyland, and Chutes and Ladders. And for dinner, serve Spaghetti-Ohs.

Want to try something other than a paper greeting card? Express yourself on video. Record and send a "video card" or "video invitation."

Empty your dull closets and go shopping at vintage or used clothing stores.

Don't worry about it, I've got

more money to burn

Here's money to REALLY burn. Take a new credit card and "max" it out on a single date. Hey, you only go around once!

Live on a wing and a prayer. Go for an airplane ride in a single-engine plane. Check out smaller air strips. Fly for a couple of hours, see the countryside, and try to spot your homes.

Amuse yourself at a traveling carnival. Go through the haunted house, ride the Ferris wheel and bumper cars, and of course, don't miss the tunnel of love.

Connect a face to the message next time you go on-line with each other. Invest in Connectix cameras and hold a private video conference with each other.

Build an aquarium. Design exotic scenery and buy a pair of exotic, tropical fish. If your relationship tanks, flush them free! (No, we're not quitting our day jobs.)

Support your local artists. Attend a local art festival or crafts fair.

Explore holistic New Age healing. Try acupuncture together to relieve the stress of it all.

Go once! Go twice! Attend an auction and bid. Sold!

Dr. Frankenstein, it's bubbling! Become beermeisters and brew your own beer.

Buy tickets for a black-tie affair for your favorite charity or cause.

Ride, captain, ride, upon that mystery ship. Go to a travel agent and give her your budget and likes. Have her schedule a surprise trip for two and see where it goes.

Come on, lucky number seven! Life's a gamble, so slide into the nearest casino and try your luck. Don't lose your shirt though (or anything else for that matter); put a limit on it.

Rent a classic or expensive car and go for a drive. Tool around, you big show-offs.

Pull! Take a shot at clay pigeon shooting.

Get away, get healthy, and visit a Club Med together. Unwind and leave the real world behind.

Don't just sit there at dinner. Travel the miles and book a date on a dinner train. Woo-woo.

You've just had the best date ever, what are you gonna do now? Go to Disneyland, DisneyWorld, or Epcot Center and be the epitome of tourists.

Hear and feel some of the most powerful engines in the world at a drag car racing or NASCAR event.

Get eclectic. Go shopping together and buy the latest in retro-style clothing and home accessories. Love that lava lamp!

Maybe you're the lost Musketeers! Learn fencing for a unique sport. Touché!

You look invigorated. And you should after treating
yourselves to a day at a health spa for
massages and mud baths.

Watch your fingers. Make reservations at a Japanese
steakhouse and be entertained as the chef prepares your
meal right before your eyes.

If you really want to stretch it to the end, rent two limos
and have a race with friends. See who can go to the
most places in the allotted time.

Do some serious people watching at a Folk, H.O.R.D.E., Lollapalooza, or other music festival. Check out the second-stage acts and sideshows, not to mention the crowd.

Want to surprise your date by cleaning their place? Hire a maid to come do the job right. Have it done when you're out and about for a welcome-home surprise.

Head out on the town for a local microbrew tasting. Sample the best of locally brewed beers. Keep track of your favorites and call a cab at the end of the night.

Create your own movie mini-series. Rent an entire series such as the *Star Wars Trilogy*, *The Godfather*, *Roots*, and *Rocky*. Watch one part each night for several nights in a row. Yo, Adrian!

Bigger . . . faster . . . scarier. . . . Check out the fiercest rides and roller-coasters at any Six Flags.

A car can be used for more than getting you to work. Go together and watch a demolition derby or attend a hot-rod show.

Getting serious now that you've passed the 12-date rule? Open a joint savings account and put in a weekly allowance. Withdraw once a month to pay for a date.

Hire a really good photographer and have cool, arty photos taken of the two of you. Take a peek at the photographer's portfolio and stay away from cheesy high school senior poses!

Pin the tail on the city map. Throw darts and wherever it lands, go.

The safest way to race a car is remote control car races. Buy one for each person. Build an obstacle course and spend hours racing.

Lasso your date and head to a rodeo.

Step on it! Buy tickets to the speedway, drag races, or Monster trucks.

Never been to an alternative sporting event as spectators? Attend kick boxing, an ultimate fighting challenge, or jai alai for a start.

Escape to another dimension, at least for a little while, anyway. Try out different virtual reality games.

Money to burn and time to kill? Discover the country. Rent a Winnebago and travel the country together.

Spend the entire day sitting back at the movies. Head to the box office and buy tickets for different shows playing throughout the day. Start with a matinee and see movies until it closes. (See page 78 for an offbeat twist.)

Got a little time to kill? Do every date idea in this book and then go back to volume one to do the same thing! (Isn't this subliminal advertising?)

It's easy to come up with

ideas when there's a

change of
seasons

It's the thought that really counts. Hand-make Valentines for each other from doilies and construction paper.

Do taxes together? Sure! You have the date, April 15th. Why not make this day a little more appealing and do your tax returns together? Whoever has the bigger refund pays for your next date.

Hate spring cleaning? Make it quick, easy, and fun. Gather the group together to clean each others' places. Clean<u>ee</u> provides dinner for everyone.

Can't ride a motorcycle? Go four-wheeling on a
four-wheeler or ATV.

Spruce up your house or apartment with a little nature.
Plant window boxes together or buy some exotic plants
from a garden center.

On a rainy day, cover your storm drains with cardboard
and play in the rainwater. Splish! Splash!

Visit an aquarium or Sea World.

Annette? Gidget? Frankie? Are you ready for your own
beach BBQ?!

Free boat ride! Sign up to crew together
at a local marina.

Do you want to catch your date hook, line, and sinker?
Go fishing together. There are a lot of fish in the sea, but
only one has to be a keeper.

Like to be a little more active in your fishing?
Try fly fishing.

Nothing like competition to bring you together.
Enter a mixed doubles tennis tournament.
Be sure to practice for it. LOVE–30.

Glub . . . glub . . . glub . . . finda zome clear water,
do zome sznorkeling, and look at zee fishes.
Say hi to Jacques for us.

Are you par for the course? Play a round of golf. Take
lessons or join a league. Here, let me help you
with your grip.

Cool off with a Slip 'n Slide or inflatable pool while you hang outside in the sun.

Need a refreshing splash? Do some pool hopping at apartment complexes or hotels. Just don't go too many times or they might get suspicious.

Party with the posh and hang with the upper crusty at a boating regatta. Ooh, you're so fabu!

I do, you do, SEA DOO! Rent a WaveRunner or water craft for two and hit the waves on a hot summer day.

Is it safe to go in the water yet? Become certified scuba divers together.

As a couple, create your own traditions for *traditional* holidays. Plan ahead of time. Be creative and don't forget them next year!

Celebrate all holidays listed on your daily planners. Happy Anzac Day to you all! (Australia)

Take a swing at an outdoor winter game. Play paddleball.

Celebrate the holidays together by fixing dinner and opening gifts before the actual day to avoid interfering with family obligations.

Dress up in costumes and hand out candy to the little goblins who come to your door for Halloween. Boo!

Throw a Halloween costume party complete with dry ice, bobbing for apples, and those gross "blind feel" boxes filled with grapes for eyeballs, cold spaghetti for brains, etc.

Don't think fishing can be cool? Try ice fishing.

Bundle up and go sledding or tobogganing. Dash through
the snow in a one-horse, open sleigh.
Oh, what fun it is . . .

Write messages in the snow using your boot tracks.
(Just your boot tracks, guys.)

Go snowmobiling.

Help prevent those winter blues. Tape record sounds of summer such as birds chirping, kids swimming, and rain falling. Then play it back in the winter.

Slip, slide, and try to stay on your feet as you play a few rounds of curling or broom ball.

Visit a tree farm and pick out the perfect Christmas tree.

Go Christmas caroling with a group of friends or family. Sing in your neighborhood or at a children's center. Fa-la-la-la-la, la-la-la-la.

Build a gingerbread house. Or better yet, eat a gingerbread house.

For a mondo bizarro twist, go Christmas caroling with a group of friends at the zoo. Sing to the animals. Now who's looking at whom?!

What's Christmas without candy?! Make chocolates from holiday molds and melted chocolate or hand-dip your own pretzels.

Get into the holiday spirit and decorate Christmas cookies together.

Watch the Christmas "A" list together—*Rudolph*, *The Grinch*, *Frosty*, and *It's a Wonderful Life*.

At Christmas, buy tickets to see a local church choir's performance of Handel's *Messiah*.

Have trouble keeping personal resolutions? List New Year's Resolutions as a couple and keep your relationship on track.

Sometimes I like dates

more
that are

group
gatherings

Pick a number and make it a party. How about a "20s" party. Invite 20 people. Hold it on the 20th of the month. Have guests dress as '20s flappers and gangsters in pinstripes.

It's an April Fool's Dinner Party. Set up a menu using numbers or code words in place of the real food names. Each guest selects 3 at a time for each course in the order to be served. The courses can be quite amusing. Appetizers could be green beans, ice cream, and no utensils.

Dig it. Have a clambake.

Take a dance on the wild side and head for your nearest
all-night or underground party. Partake of smart drinks
and mosh away.

Host a Bad Taste Party that's all in good fun. Cover the
furniture with plastic, hang black velvet paintings,
and dress in bad taste costumes.

For the ultimate in private parties, rent out
an entire bar for the night.

Hi, Bob! It's a Bob Newhart Party! Assign a specific character to each guest. When the character appears on the show or action occurs have rules that the guest must do like stand up and sing, stand on your head, drink a beer, or do the chicken dance.

Now you can wear the plaid with the paisley. At a Nerds Party everyone is welcome! Next month the sequel, Revenge of the Nerds Party.

Grab the gang, cram in the car, and head out on a group road trip.

Bowling's getting moody. Check your local lanes for some midnight bowling. Alleys are lit using only candles or flashlights.

So you thought you'd never wear it again . . . have a Bridesmaid Dress Revisited Party. Dig deep into your closet and pull out the formal gown you were forced to wear in a wedding. Serve cocktails. Oh, that big satin bow . . . it's <u>really</u> you!

Yuppies, BMWs, and Perrier. Relive the glory years and era of conspicuous consumption. Throw an '80s Party.

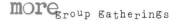

Throw a Celebrity-Look-Alike Party and impersonate your favorite stars. Now, who do you look like?

So, Dad used to chomp on one and Mom got a little tipsy with just a few sips—lounge at a cigar bar and sip a few choice martinis.

Dress with an attitude. Hit the town and do some clubbing. Find the hottest nightclubs and stay up all night. Check out those club kids!

Belly up to the bar. Have a creative cocktail making and tasting party. Bring various ingredients and concoct new drinks you can name after your friends.

You may wish you were both color-blind at a Color Party. If you pick red, everyone wears red, all food is red, paint the walls red, etc.

Not feeling very active tonight? It's okay, just be couch potatoes. Watch TV, share the remote, order in pizza, etc. You go, you big spud!

Howdy pardner. Saddle up and host a Country Hoe-down Party, complete with watermelon seed spitting, cow chip tossing, and BBQ ribs on the grill.

Get off your butts and play a game of dodge ball. Ouch, not in the face!

Our fellow members of the Order of Sacred Bullmooses and Bovines . . . create your own fraternal group with your friends. Devise your own set of traditions, rituals, handshake, etc. Have T-shirts made and go on monthly group outings.

Host a "Friday the 13th" Party. The date is already set (duh). Make guests enter under a ladder, break mirrors, spill salt, and perform other bad-luck superstitions. Of course one of the movies should be playing.

Who's the maddest hatter of them all? Throw a Hat Party and find out. Admission is one wild hat.

Get away for a day. Gather your friends, chip in, and rent a houseboat or yacht. Have a party and enjoy the day swimming, fishing, sailing, whatever.

Have a Kitchen Gadget Night. Invite friends over and
have them bring their one-purpose-only gift gadgets and
other useless thingamajigs along with the food that goes
with them. Use them all to see what interesting dinner
courses you come up with.

It may not be down under but you can get down. Have a
Mad Max Party. Guests dress in car parts or ruffian
outfits. Serve Australian fare.

Strike a pose at a Model Party. Guests are announced,
strobes flash, and music pumps as they walk the entry
"runway." Too sexy.

There you are . . . show your stuff at a Miss Universe Party. Everyone attends in old prom dresses, sequin dresses, or formal wear and performs a hidden talent. Everyone judges for the best performance. Award door prizes and *booby* prizes. (Oops, how'd that get in here?)

Remember all those night games you played as a kid? They're just as fun as adults. Play classics like Kick the Can, Hide-n-Seek, or Ghosts in the Graveyard. (Allee, allee, something and something free.)

Don't just hang at one bar, go on an impromptu pub crawl. Check please.

Hold an Oscar Party and arrive in style. Black tie and formal wear are the fashion of the night. Cast your predictions for Hollywood's winners. Make it a contest. Celebrate the outcomes throughout the night.

Polka dots . . . flannel . . . cotton . . . tighty whities. See what your friends wear to bed and host a Pajama Party. Stay up reading bedtime stories, serve cookies and milk, or rent *House Party*.

Take on whole new characters. Try a role-playing game like Advanced Dungeons and Dragons, Shadowrun, Rifts, and Dragonlance: Fifth Age.

Afraid that you're becoming your parents? Don't be! You are, at least for a night, if you throw a Dress Like Your Parents Party. Have guests dress and act as their Mom or Dad. Make it a contest. Nice polyester!

Invite friends and charter a bus for your pub crawl. Map out your bar and club destinations beforehand. Call ahead of time to see if you can arrange any group food or drink specials.

Wear old sheets and host a classic "Animal House Toga Party." Don't forget the Jell-O shots.

Sensory overload! Have a Sensory Party with a variety of smells, tastes, sights, and sounds. Burn incense for more smell, serve spicy foods for taste, play music for sound, and cover your furniture with velvets for touch. Use your imagination.

You know the story of *Stone Soup*. Create a Soup Party. Require your guests to bring one ingredient of their choice. Combine, stir, and heat for a hopefully tasty treat.

Bring back your date's deepest, darkest secrets or most embarrassing moments with a "This Is Your Life" Birthday Party. Call their family and friends for the dirt.

Bond . . . James Bond. Dust off your tuxedos and formal wear for a James Bond Spy Party. Rent your favorite thrillers. Assign a "murderer." Try to figure out who it is before they get you.

Touchdown! Host a Super Bowl Party with chili and barbecue. Rent a big-screen TV. You're sure to win so long as you don't fumble the bowl . . . or ball?

Mirror, mirror, on the wall, who's the ugliest of us all? Organize an Ugly Dance! Guests mismatch clothes, mess up hair, cake on the makeup, and just get uuugleee!

All together now! *Everyone* chips in $3 to buy ingredients for good group foods like tacos, burritos, or pizza. *Everyone* goes to the grocery store to shop. *Everyone* helps prepare the meal. And everyone cleans up. Does *everyone* got it?

And one more plug . . . another buzz boxx book, buy *The Host-with-the-Most Handbook of Party Ideas*, that details more group gathering ideas. You'll certainly be "the host with the most."

thank you

We just wanted to say thanks to everyone who provided additional dating ideas for this book:

Debbie Bornhuetter, Kenosha, WI; Meagn Goose, Loveland, OH; Conna Graham, Peachtree City, GA; Garrie and Georgia Hainer, Muskego, WI; Jill Holbert, Carmel, IN; Christine Jeschke, Indianapolis, IN; Matt Keedy, Indianapolis, IN; Teri Kinder, Indianapolis, IN; Greg Matsunami, Portland, OR; Shawn Peters, Indianapolis, IN; Christine Provencher, Whitefish Bay, WI; Karen Riese, Appleton, WI; Laura Rossiter, Indianapolis, IN; Joy Rowe, Loveland, OH; Kathy Sathre, Union City, CA; Bob Schewe, Chicago, IL; Claire Simpson, Chicago, IL; Aaron Spielberg, Fort Lee, NJ; Rich Stoddart, Minneapolis, MN; Starla Tohline, Madeira, OH; April Ward, Carmel, IN; and Kathy Wendell, Indianapolis, IN.

Special thanks to all these very cool people who posed for photos for the book. (Didn't your parents tell you not to talk to strangers?) They are:

Jessica Adams, Michelle Alexander, Stephanie Arzigian, Andrew Balen, Lori Benedict, Dee Dee Benkie, Steven Boad, Candice Broadus, Marie Brown, Kelly Bruner, Aimée Calmes, Brett Carlile, Kate Carr, Torenzo Chestnut, Delanna Cody, Jacobia Coluter, Eric Cotter, Brandon Daugherty, Bradford James Davis, Eric Dearth, Jong Durables, Brian Ellis, M. Everett, Michelle Gabriel, Jennifer Garrison, Todd Gresley, Kelley Hahn, Janeen Hawkins, Jana Haynes, Jill Haynes, Andrea Heilman, LaRanette Hillman, Stuart Hudson, Motoko Imai, Delana Ivey, Eduardo Jimenez, Heather Johnson, Jeremy Johnson,

Clayton Jordan III, Jeremiah Kortz, Londell Marina, Martina Martens, Dusty McMillan, Kristen McMullen, Alice Marie Moherlo, Angela Mullenix, Abdou N'Diaye, Derek Neumeier, Nathan Nunn, Patrick Peacock, Michelle Peccia, Jason Penn, Kari Perkins, Christine Pierce, N. Pinede, Jocelyn Rasnick, Marhia Ross, Anne St. Aubin, Emily Schafer, Brian Schweitzer, Steven Sippy, La'Shay Slaughter, DeWayne Smith, Bryan Stevenson, Sheila Sutton, Jon Swartz, Maria Sonia Tansinsin, Bruce Wadlington, Heather Waterman, and Desiree Yaroush.

You all were great!

GCBB seeks EMDI
for good times, maybe even more.

That's Group Called Buzz Boxx seeks EVEN MORE Dating Ideas. Yep, we're moving onto *The Little Black Book of EVEN MORE Dating Ideas, Volume 3* and welcome more dating ideas from all you love gods and goddesses. You know the drill, send any new or interesting dating ideas along with your name and address to us at:

buzz boxx

P.O. Box 40671

Indianapolis, IN 46240-0671

or e-mail us at:

buzzboxx@aol.com (don't forget the second "x.")

And the legal stuff—if you do submit an idea, you understand you are willingly sending it to us, you're over 18, you're releasing all rights to it, you're giving us permission to use it any way we want, including that we may or may not attribute your idea to you by name or use a fictitious name . . . blah, blah, blah. (Dave and Russell, our lawyers, get uptight if we don't add this stuff. We think they could use a long vacation.)

Psssst . . . one more thing. Andrews and McMeel didn't want us to tell you this but we will personally send you a FREE copy of Volume 3 on behalf of buzz boxx if we use your idea in it. Please don't tell them we told you. You know how uptight English majors can be.

more buzz boxx books

Hey you! This is our blatant attempt to sell more books! Did you know that we have other buzz boxx books besides this one? Look for these buzz boxx titles at cooler stores everywhere:

1 *The Little Black Book of Dating Ideas*

2 *The Little Black Book of MORE Dating Ideas, Volume 2*

3 *Pick-Up Lines™: The Best and Worst on Planet Earth*

Oh, and if you can't find these at your favorite stores, put the full court press on the store owner or manager to order copies of these books. Sometimes they just don't "get it" because they don't understand our generation.